Leadership ✻ Network

THE LEGACY OF A
HER⚡O
MAKER

DAVE FERGUSON
AND TODD WILSON

FOREWORD BY RON EDMONDSON

A SUPPLEMENTAL RESOURCE TO THE BOOK
HERO MAKER

Dedicated to Bob Buford, a true hero maker

DEDICATION

The teams at Leadership Network and Exponential worked together to dedicate this book to the life and memory of Bob Buford, a true hero maker! Bob passed into the arms of Jesus on April 18, 2018, and certainly heard his Master say, "Well done good and faithful servant!"

SPECIAL NOTE

This book is a collection and integration of numerous articles, blog posts, and podcast interviews written by Dave Ferguson and Todd Wilson during the past year. These articles were written to support the 2018 Exponential theme book *Hero Maker: Five Essential Practices for Leader to Multiply Leaders*. In integrating these articles into a single book resource, we've sought to preserve the voice of the authors. As such, parts of the content are written from the first-person perspective of each author. Where appropriate, we indicate which author is speaking.

ACKNOWLEDGEMENTS

This book is a supplemental resource to the book *Hero Maker: Five Essential Practices for Leaders to Multiply Leaders* by Dave Ferguson and Warren Bird. We are grateful to the team at Harper Collins Publishing for enthusiastically supporting this supplemental resource.

Bob Buford, founder of Leadership Network, passed into the arms of Jesus earlier this year. Bob was a true hero maker who personally impacted Dave and Todd, and their respective ministries. This book is dedicated to Bob's life and the legacy he built by modeling hero making for an entire generation of church leaders. Bob always said, "my fruit grows on other people's trees." This signature saying should be the heartbeat of hero makers everywhere. Thank you, Bob!

Lindy Lowry, our longtime, friend and amazing editor is the one who takes pages upon pages of text and pulls it together into something readable. Thank you, Lindy. The rest of the Exponential Team also takes care of all the behind-the-scenes details to make it possible for free resources like this one to be distributed.

Our friends and partners in ministry at Leadership Network are co-publishing this resource. They've been such a blessing to the Church and the diffusion of innovation to accelerate the impact of churches. The same "you can do it, how can we help" culture that Bob Buford built into their DNA has been carried forward to Exponential and so many other ministries.

Warren Bird (co-author with Dave of Hero Maker: Five Essential Practices for Leaders to Multiply Leaders) was instrumental in helping research and formulate the five essential practices. Warren's keen insights and diligence were instrumental in the development of the Hero Maker library of resources.

≡XPONENTIAL⌐

RESOURCING CHURCH PLANTERS

- 90+ eBooks
- Largest annual church planting conference in the world (Exponential Global Event in Orlando)
- Regional Conferences - Boise, DC, Southern CA, Bay Area CA, Chicago, Houston and New York City
- Exponential Español (spoken in Spanish)
- FREE Online Multiplication & Mobilization Assessments
- FREE Online Multiplication & Mobilization Courses
- Conference content available via Digital Access Pass (Training Videos)
- Weekly Newsletter
- 1000+ Hours of Free Audio Training
- 100s of Hours of Free Video Training
- Free Podcast Interviews

exponential.org

Twitter.com/churchplanting
Facebook.com/churchplanting
Instagram.com/church_planting

INSIDE

FOREWORD

Every day I serve at Leadership Network, I hear a new story of the impact Bob Buford has had on someone or some church or organization. Sometimes that impact is through one of our many pastor groups; other times, it's because someone read his book, *Halftime*, or attended one of Halftime Institute's events.

Or it might be through one of the dozens of ministries and organizations that have grown from a spark ignited by something Bob invested in either financially or with his time, energy and counsel. Regardless of the vehicle of impact, one thing is for certain: Bob Buford's legacy will continue to be lived out in the lives of people for many years and decades to come.

The amazing thing that strikes me about these stories is that most of these leaders never actually met Bob Buford. They may or may not even know his name. They simply benefited from something or someone who Bob impacted through the things he did and the way he lived his life.

I understand, because I'm one of those stories. The ministry of Leadership Network helped me as a pastor when we were trying to figure out some critical next steps at our church. The relationships with other pastors in the pastor leader groups I was a part of have had a lifetime impact on me. Yet I only met Bob in the hallway a couple of times. He wouldn't have likely known my name.

I can't think of a better example of a Hero Maker than Bob Buford. As Bob said, and it's repeated frequently in our offices, "My fruit grows on other people's trees." The Kingdom needs more hero makers. We need pastors and planters and business people and church attendees who willingly invest their time and treasures into bearing fruit they might never personally see.

My prayer is that this book—and the movement of organizations like Exponential and Leadership Network and others—will spur even more people to live their life like Bob Buford, encouraging even more Kingdom-building hero makers to come.

—Ron Edmondson, *CEO of Leadership Network*

INTRODUCTION

An Introduction to Hero Making

Who doesn't want to be a hero? Heroes are celebrated for their courageous acts, special achievements, and noble character. Deep down, we all long to live lives bigger than ourselves. We're naturally drawn to the hero role.

Think about it. When you watch movies, my guess is you rarely see yourself in the shoes of the villain or even the supporting cast. Instead, we're drawn to the life of the superhero, putting ourselves at the center of the main plot.

I (Todd) will be the first to admit I want to be the hero of the story. Being the hero feels good. But over the years, I've learned that there is an even better role to aspire to than "hero." A role that shifts my focus from addition to multiplication, and from "me" to "others."

Ultimately, a shift that makes me (and anyone who makes this shift) much more like Jesus!

Behind Every Hero

Have you ever thought that heroes are made? Every hero has a hero maker—a mom or dad, a friend, a co-worker, a teacher, a coach, or you and me.

Think of Barnabas, the hero maker to Paul and many others. The scales had barely fallen from Paul's eyes before Barnabas had taken him to the apostles and vouched for him. Later, he took Paul to the Antioch church, ultimately setting him up for planting churches that would advance the cross and change the world. Barnabas shifted from hero to becoming the mentor who creates hero makers that ultimately become mentors (i.e., Paul to Timothy).

Hero makers like Barnabas have a pattern of investing in others to see the full potential of others released into others. (Say that five times fast.) Essentially, they are disciple makers who make disciple makers. Their scorecards are measured not by what they do, but rather by how they release the potential in others.

Here's the paradox. If we focus on being a hero, we may do some great things on this side of eternity. However, if we focus on being a hero maker, we'll see great things happen through the people we invest in and the people they invest in and so on. Paradoxically, hero makers on earth become heroes in eternity. Can you imagine the crazy long line of people in Heaven who are smiling at Bob Buford, saying, *Thank you… because of you, I'm here. …Because of your investment, I followed Christ. …Because of your influence, I led others here.*

The Ultimate Hero Maker

Of course, Jesus is the ultimate hero and hero maker. Christ invested in us, through His death, so that the best of what God intended for us could be redeemed and made whole. When Jesus said, "The greatest among you will be your servant," He was talking about making hero makers. He modeled it in how He lived. And since He modeled it, He expects it of us!

Jesus has called us to be hero makers, also through how we live, because He knows that if we're going to follow His Great Commission to make disciples, we will need to be hero makers. Back in 2016, when my (Todd) wife, Anna, first saw that Exponential's theme was "HeroMaker," her heart skipped a beat.

"I'm not a national leader or church planter," she told me, "but I can invest in making someone else better and helping release their full potential."

Hero making is accessible to every follower of Jesus because Jesus, Himself, is every disciple's hero maker. We are all capable and called to be hero makers who sacrificially invest in others with what Bob Buford consistently referred to as "permission, encouragement, and applause."

Imagine the impact if each day we sincerely asked ourselves, "Who can I invest in to make a hero maker today?"

Hero Making and Level 5 Multiplication

It would seem that church planting would require a hero—a leader who's going to take the leap to make things happen. But we've discovered that the catalytic church planting that's going to start or be part of a Level 5 multiplying Kingdom movement requires what we've been talking about. Level 5 multiplication is depending on how well we become hero makers.

Every true shift in a church or organization begins with a heart change in the primary leader. Marked by a sense of holy and humble tenacity, multiplying leaders shift from being simply the hero of their church to helping others become the hero makers and the future mentors the church will need. In fact, our friend and multiplier Ralph Moore is the first to say that multiplication lives and dies on leaders who are willing to pass the baton and empower others to lead.

Level 5 multiplication must be led by hero-making leaders who are passionate about creating and maintaining a biblical culture of multiplication. We desperately need hero makers to emerge who can catalyze movements of Level 5 multiplying churches.

How else will we move from being addition heroes of our story to multiplication hero makers of God's story?

What to Expect

In this book, we're looking at what a hero maker looks like and unpacking the practices of hero makers with a special focus on Bob Buford who died this past year. You'll be able to take Exponential's FREE HeroMaker assessment (funded by Bob's generosity), which measures your personal multiplication leadership capacity.

You'll be hearing from Todd Wilson and Dave Ferguson (co-author with Warren Bird of the groundbreaking book *Hero Maker: Five Essential Practices for Leaders to Multiply Leaders*[1]) who were both personally and significantly impacted by Bob's modeling of hero making. Throughout the book, Dave and Todd will both be sharing their stories and insights. You'll also find reflection questions at the end of each chapter as well as a practical and simple "tool" you can use to help you start to implement each of these practices in your own life and ministry. These proven tools come from the *Hero Maker* book, and we're excited about sharing them with you in these pages.

For several months, we've been writing and talking about these five practices. This book is the culmination of all of our efforts to start, shape and steward this conversation. Ultimately, our hope and prayer are that it will be one of those go-to resources that you can (and will) come back to over and over as you embark and stay on the lifelong journey of becoming a hero maker.

CHAPTER 1

Bob Buford: Leaving a Hero-Making Legacy

We lost a giant of a man this year—one of the most unsung Christian hero makers of our generation.

You might know Bob Buford best as the author of the best-selling book *Halftime*.[2] But Bob was also an entrepreneur and philanthropist behind numerous ministries that have strengthened thousands of church leaders and the Church at large. He leaves behind a living legacy that includes the impact of Halftime Institute, Exponential and Leadership Network, among numerous others.

We have no doubt that on April 18, 2018, Jesus was there to embrace Bob with the words we all hope to hear: "Well done good and faithful servant." The mosaic of stories in eternity with a connection to this quiet movement maker is simply profound. In fact, Bob kept a "Book of Days" (actually 10-plus volumes) with notes, letters, cards, and articles that people sent him saying, "Thank you, Bob for …." His primary legacy comes through the people he invested in who would, in turn, propel his values forward to others and multiply this DNA.

When we think about what it means and looks like to be a hero maker, it's natural for our thoughts to immediately turn to Bob. Like a true hero maker, Bob never wanted or sought the limelight. Instead, he championed others to succeed for the sake of the Kingdom. He lived out the words he became known for, such as, "I'm the catapult; you're the plane," "You can do it, how can I help?" and, "My fruit grows on other people's trees." He simply wanted to do for others what his mentor, (father of modern management) Peter Drucker, did for him.

And like Peter Drucker modeled, Bob focused on coming alongside others and giving them permission and encouragement to be and do all that God made them for. He did this in his personal and professional life. Bob was so laser-focused in his approach and in his love and respect for the three most important people in his life: Jesus Christ his Lord, his wife Linda, and Peter Drucker.

Bob also cared deeply about the future of American Christianity and wanted to leverage every one unit of input effort (dollars, effort or intellectual capital) into 100 units of output results. He was burdened by what he called, "100x Kingdom impact." Those units could be church plants, shoes on kids, or marketplace leaders moving from success to significance.

In short, his mission was to transform the latent capacity of American Christianity into active energy. And he did that by investing in others who also cared deeply about the future of American Christianity. He frequently said, "There is more to giving than feeling good. The joy is found in the results of transformed lives."

From Ideas to Action to Exponential Impact

Of course, the real test of a hero maker comes down to their fruit. Are the values they're teaching and living out taking root in others?

At Exponential, we've seen thousands of leaders take eternity-altering steps to plant churches and start networks of multiplying churches. As we talk about hero making that leads to multiplication, it's only right that the footprint of a hero maker like Bob's would be part of Exponential's DNA and story. In part, Exponential's 2018 HeroMaker theme stems from Bob's example. His fruit grows on our trees. Specifically, his "you can do it; how can we help?" value is embedded into our values and culture.

Leadership Network is literally the footprint of a hero maker enabled by Bob's half-time call to move from success to significance. When given the challenge to articulate the one thing that he wanted to make the greatest difference with in his life, Bob narrowed his initial response, including both continued success in business and Kingdom results, to the latter—investing in the people and initiatives that would accelerate Kingdom impact.

He initially framed the "how can we help?" question in this manner: "What is the greatest need in the Church today that no one else is meeting?" The answer—resourcing the leaders of the emerging movement of what has now come to be known as the megachurch—led Bob to begin to gather these leaders, creating an environment for their ideas to be shaped in ways that led to action and ultimately exponential impact. Impact so significant that Peter Drucker came to believe that the institution having the greatest transformative influence on the culture in the late 20th and early 21st century was the large local church. Bob's investment in leaders was an investment in hero makers.

Another characteristic of hero makers is their focus on others. Bob had a relentless focus on others from the beginning of Leadership Network. He stated it early and often through the operating principle that guided our work: "We are called to be the platform, not the show." The players on stage have been, and always will be, the pastors and leaders Leadership Network served. Bob's commitment to hero making continues to shape the values and culture of Leadership Network.

An Abundance of Fruit

Bob's immeasurable influence and impact are just a few of the reasons why Leadership Network is honored to partner with Exponential in the dedication all of the 2018 Hero Maker events and this book to him. You'll find stories about Bob and his insights woven throughout these chapters, as well as the epigraphs opening the chapters.

Our hope and belief are that as we look to Bob's example and birth hero makers who multiply disciples, churches and ultimately, the Kingdom of God, this book will be part of Bob's (and your) living legacy—and an abundance of more of his fruit growing on countless trees.

Thank you, Bob, for finishing well and leaving a living legacy through the hero makers you've made. It goes without saying that Bob Buford embodied and demonstrated all five of the hero-making practices we're sharing about in this resource. By unpacking them and doing for others what Bob did for thousands, we honor and celebrate his life and impact.

CHAPTER 2

Measuring What Matters

"My fruit grows on other people's trees."

~Bob Buford

Of course, a huge part of how effective you'll be at hero making relies on your scorecard and what you're measuring. The personal scorecards of hero makers are measured not by what *they* do, but rather by how they release the potential in others.

Bob's death has me (Todd) thinking a lot about that. Contributing to this season of reflection is the realization that I've now been in vocational ministry for more years than I spent in the marketplace as a nuclear engineer—and I likely have less working years ahead of me than I've left behind.

Additionally, writing and talking about being a hero maker frequently has me asking myself hard and challenging questions: *Am I motivated primarily by becoming the hero in the center of my story, or am I giving the best of myself to becoming the hero maker of others in God's unfolding story?*

If that's not enough, add two years of dealing with two different medical conditions that could have (or should have) killed me. All these things have naturally prompted questions about legacy and measuring what's really important in life.

Maybe you're in a similar place. Maybe, like me, you're asking yourself: *Am I being the best possible steward of the time, talents, and treasures that God has blessed me with?*

Am *I focused primarily on pursuing a legacy by* **what** *I build, accumulate and leave behind, or by* **who** *I invest in and catapult forward to the next generation?*

We could summarize all of these questions more succinctly: *Am I measuring here on earth what matters most on the scorecard of eternity?*

People Matter!

On a recent vacation to the beach (mine and Anna's happy place), I spent the week resting, reading, reflecting, and recharging. I kept things simple and brought my Bible, one book, and a journal. Throughout the week, a theme gradually but clearly emerged: "The investment in people matters!"

Let me explain.

First, I had intended to read through the entire New Testament and journal what the Holy Spirit was whispering to me. I started in the Book of Acts but never made it any farther. Instead, I dwelled on this one book of "action" all week. My journal notes ended up being longer than the book itself.

This isn't the first time I've read Acts, by any means. Each time I read it, I'm always energized by the same thing—the intersection of the mission-centric pioneering spirit of the apostles and the faith-saturated surrender stories that catalyzed the greatest movement in the history of mankind. The apostle Paul is an inspiration for all Kingdom-minded monomaniac-wannabes like me. Acts is our inspirational pep talk!

But this time, something was different. Page after page, I was struck not by the pioneering spirit but instead by the people stories. Not necessarily the heroes in each chapter but instead by the supporting cast members that I've easily skimmed over in the past. You see, I've always read Acts with Paul as the hero in the center of his unfolding entrepreneurial journey and story.

If I'm being really transparent, I've always seen myself in Paul's shoes as the hero of the story. This time, however, I read Acts with Jesus as the ultimate hero and hero maker in Paul's story and Paul as a missionary hero maker and supporting cast member. That different vantage point shifts the focus from events and impact to people and investments.

Yes, Paul boldly and obediently pioneered three missionary journeys; carried the gospel to the Gentiles; wrote much of the New Testament; and planted the gospel in all kinds of new places. But his lasting impact that actually reaches out and touches us today through our spiritual lineage is found in the mosaic of people Paul invested in, encouraged and ultimately catapulted forward 2,000 years ago.

Paul was the hero maker of Timothy, Silas, Cornelius, Lydia, Aquila, Priscilla, and countless others who, in turn, became hero makers. And we are their beneficiaries. The question is, "Will we follow in their footsteps and do the same, becoming hero makers to the next generation?"

Don't miss the focus on investing in people!

The Hidden Secret to Legacy Impact

A second thing happened on this beach getaway. Of the hundreds of books on my radar, John Doerr's new book, *Measure What Matters,*[3] made it to the top of my reading list. John Doerr is the chairman of the venture capital firm Kleiner Perkins Caufield & Byers (KPCB), considered by many to be the world's best venture capital platform. Doerr and KPCB helped companies like Google, Facebook, and Amazon get their starts.

With KPCB's portfolio of over 800 of the top startups in U.S. history, John easily captured my attention with his new book. His approach to setting objectives and seeing key results (what he calls OKRs) is simultaneously simple and powerful.

Every few pages, I would tell Anna what a great book it is. But the core message and focus of his book wasn't what captured me. Instead, I was mostly inspired and intrigued by the backstory of Doerr's relationship with two mentors, Andy Grove and Bill Campbell. I have no idea if these men were Christians, but they certainly were hero makers in his life. Their examples in Doerr's life show the profound impact of a simple investment in other people—an investment that's easily taken for granted. Let me summarize it.

Andy Grove was the CEO of Intel in the 1980s. He was certainly what we'd call a "monomaniac on a mission." In Doerr's words, he knew "what he wanted, how to get it, and was driven by an urgency and focus to attain it."[4] Bill Campbell was a coach to some of the best business executives and teams, including Google founders Larry Page and Sergey Brin.

The role that Grove and Campbell played in mentoring Doerr reveals the hidden secret to legacy impact. These two men were responsible for helping build some of the most important and impactful companies in the world and in shaping the landscape of technology. Yes, they accumulated and left amazing things behind. But the real multiplying impact of their work is through the hundreds of thousands of leaders they invested in, shaped, and catapulted beyond themselves.

Bill Campbell died of cancer two years ago. Doerr included a special dedication to his mentor's legacy, writing: "Bill Campbell was always a players' coach. [Now, it's] my chance to become a player coach for the next generation of leaders and partners. To follow Bill's lead. Bill is gone, but for his many hundreds of disciples, all the executives he coached over all those years, his work goes on."[5]

Doerr could have highlighted a monumental list of profound accomplishments in Campbell's life. He could have made the case for a legacy characterized by accumulation and impact. Instead, he highlighted his most significant legacy: He was a hero maker. Doerr's most significant testimony of Campbell's legacy is found in his desire to "do for others what Bill had done for him."

That's what Bob Buford always said. Many times, I heard Bob passionately say he "wanted to do for others what Peter Drucker (his mentor) did for him." I was one of those beneficiaries. Like Doerr, I now want to do for others what Bob did for me.

Most importantly, I want to pass Bob's values for hero making to others and practice, like Bob did with me and countless leaders, coming alongside others with intentionality (connecting), helping them see beyond the fog and clouds that surround them (clarifying), and helping launch them forward beyond the fog (accelerating).

These actions are the secret to a legacy so much greater than what we accumulate and leave behind. They are the keys to focusing on "who" we catapult forward beyond ourselves rather than "what" we accumulate and leave behind on this earth. As we invest in others, measuring what matters, we begin to make this critical shift for multiplication.

Making It Personal

- *If you're honest, what role do you truly want to play? Hero or hero maker?*
- *How do you want your legacy to be formed? Are you building a legacy primarily on accumulation and accomplishment or investment in others?*
- *What role do you believe God wants you to play? Why?*
- *Who was your hero maker?*
- *How did he or she invest in you and make you the hero?*
- *Who are you catapulting? If no one, who in your path can you invest in and catapult?*

CHAPTER 3

The Practices of a Hero Maker

"You can do it, how can I help?"

–Bob Buford

As a kid, I (Todd) never aspired to be in the military though my career path eventually took me there. Growing up, I do remember wearing my Superman cape with intentions of saving the world from evil.

"Faster than a speeding bullet, more powerful than a locomotive, able to leap tall buildings in a single bound, powers and abilities far beyond mortal men, changing the course of mighty rivers, bending steel in my bare hands, and fighting a never-ending battle for truth, justice, and the American way."

Although I knew I'd never become the next Superman, deep down I longed to be a hero. We all do. But as we talked about in the last chapter, there's an even better role. However, that role doesn't come naturally. To become hero makers, we have to be intentional.

Shifting Our Motives, Methods, and Measures

By now, you know that change doesn't come easy. Shedding the Superman cape and moving from hero to hero maker requires at least three shifts. We must shift our motives, methods and measures of success. Let's look at each one:

- *Motives* – Shifting from a "me-centric" motive to an "others-biased" motive, rooted in making the name of Jesus more famous rather than our own. Hell is real, Heaven is now, and our motives must be rooted in the truth that people matter to God. The mission has urgency, and the consequences impact eternity.
- *Methods (focus)* – We must shift our approach from, "I can do it; you can help" to an approach rooted in what Bob always said: "You can do it; how can I help?" Our priority must shift from **what** we accomplish, accumulate, and leave behind to **who** we invest in and catapult forward beyond us.
- *Measures of success* – We must shift our scorecard measures from addition thinking to multiplication thinking, from numbers on earth to people in Heaven, and from our empire to God's Kingdom.

Five Practices in Hero Making: An Overview

As we've worked through what it means to be a hero maker, in addition to these three shifts we've also identified five specific characteristics of this kind of leader: multiplication thinker; permission giver; disciple multiplier; gift activator; and Kingdom builder. These values continually show up as leadership values in everything hero makers do.

In the research for their groundbreaking book, *Hero Maker: Five Essential Practices for Leaders to Multiply Leaders,*[6] Dave Ferguson and Warren Bird, stress that these five practices derive from the characteristics we see in the life and ministry of Jesus and in the leadership of contemporary hero makers.

As Warren and I (Dave) looked at Jesus' life in the Gospels, we saw hero making consistently lived out in Jesus' life and ministry. His death on the cross was heroic. He stretched out His arms and said, "Not my will, but yours be done" (Luke 22:42). He invested in us, through His death, so that the best of what God intended for us could be redeemed and made whole.

But Jesus didn't stop there. He made hero makers out of his closest followers. Jesus was pretty explicit about His desire to equip His followers to do the heroic: "Very truly I tell you, whoever believes in me will do the works I have been doing, and they will do even *greater things* than these because I am going to the Father" (John 14:12, emphasis added). Jesus told the disciples that He was setting them up so that they could reach *more* people, go to *more* placcs, write a book we call the Bible, and make *more* disciples than He *ever* would during His three years of earthly ministry.

You just can't study Jesus' ministry practices without seeing Him as someone who puts the spotlight on others, who in turn do likewise for others. He modeled it in how He lived, calling us to be hero-making Level 5 multipliers.

These five hero-making practices include:

Multiplication Thinking: The first hero-making practice is a shift to multiplication thinking—a shift in *thinking*. In this practice, you move from thinking the best way to maximize ministry is through your own efforts to understanding that it actually happens through developing the leadership of others. We see this in the life of Jesus in Acts 1:8 when He casts a vision for taking the gospel to the ends of the earth and explains to His followers that He's going to do it through them: "… and you will be my witnesses." Jesus didn't think the mission would happen just though Him during His time on this earth; He knew it would happen through others who would equip others who would equip still others. Jesus practiced multiplication thinking.

Permission Giving: The second hero-making practice is permission giving—a shift in *seeing*. You take the focus off your leadership and begin to see the leadership potential in the people all around you. Looking for and identifying leadership potential in others will cause you to begin to lead with a bias to "yes" and give them permission to fully engage in the mission. We see this in the life of Jesus when He says to a group of rag-tag working-class fellows, "Come follow Me." They never expected a rabbi to see them as worthy of teaching and leading. But Jesus saw in them a group that could change the world. He not only gave them permission; He also told them they could change the world!

Disciple Multiplying: The third hero-making practice is disciple multiplying—a shift in *sharing*. You begin to share not just what you know to help others follow Jesus, but to also share your life and invest in the development of leaders who do the same for other leaders. We see this in the life of Jesus as He spent three years with primarily twelve people. Jesus spent time with the Twelve and shared His life with them, and they, in turn, multiplied themselves into a movement of Jesus followers.

Gift Activating: The fourth hero-making practice is gift activating—a shift in *blessing*. Not only do you ask God to bless the gifts He has given you, but you also ask God to bless the leaders you have developed and send out at the end of their apprenticeship. The most obvious example of this is in Matthew 28. Jesus turns over the leadership of the movement to His closest followers and tells them, in effect, "I have all authority, and will work through you as you go!" Jesus activated their leadership gifts by giving them His blessing to "go."

Kingdom Building: The last and fifth hero-making practice is Kingdom building—a shift in *counting*. You are no longer only concerned with who's showing up at *your* thing; you also count who's doing God's thing! Jesus told His followers in simple terms, "Seek first the Kingdom of God." They followed this admonition, and all that mattered was that God was keeping track of how the Jesus mission was being advanced around the world.

We've realized that when leaders cultivate and embrace all five of these characteristics, they undergo an integral shift. They move from being the hero of their own story who's focused on building their own empire to becoming a hero maker in God's unfolding story—bent on growing and advancing His Kingdom. Hero makers recognize the important role they play in identifying, encouraging, launching and multiplying disciples who multiply disciples.

This is the kind of leader the world needs to move the Church forward—and ultimately to see millions of eternities changed.

Over the next five chapters, we'll be unpacking each of these practices identified in *Hero Maker* and looking specifically at what it takes to become a hero maker who focuses on how these values play out in their lives and churches. So far, we've talked about what a hero maker is and looks like. Now here's where the proverbial rubber meets the road and we learn how to, as hero maker Bob Buford often said, "be the catapult."

Making It Personal

- *Why do you think becoming a hero maker takes intentionality?*
- *What are the primary motives and methods you need to shift to become a hero maker?*
- *How are you measuring success? Is your scorecard more addition- or multiplication-focused?*
- *List below the three primary ways you measure your success. Be transparent.*
- *Do you truly believe Jesus' words in John 14:12—that you can do greater things than Jesus? Why or why not?*
- *Think about the five practices in hero making. Based on what you know right now about these values (you'll know more after the next five chapters), who in your life has demonstrated these values?*
- *Have you ever seen someone give up the spotlight to shine the spotlight on others? What did that look like?*
- *What are the benefits and consequences of full-time paid staff being the "heroes" rather than "hero makers?" How does this impact your church's ability to move to Level 5 multiplication?*
- *In last chapter's questions, we asked you to identify potential leaders in your church. Are you releasing these people for multiplication? If so, how? If not, why not?*

CHAPTER 4

HeroMaker Practice 1: Multiplication Thinking

"I want to be remembered as the seed that was planted in good soil and multiplied a hundredfold."

~ Bob Buford

Years ago, I (Todd) asked a friend who was sightseeing in Washington D.C., what his favorite thing was to see at the American History Museum.

His answer will surprise you (it did me).

"Archie Bunker's chair from the 1970s TV sitcom *All in the Family.*"

My immediate thought was, *"That's stupid. How could a chair be your favorite thing to see when some of the most important things in our nation's history are there?*

Fast-forward two decades when I had the privilege of touring Rancho del Cielo, President Ronald Reagan's ranch in the mountains outside Santa Barbara, California. The ranch home is small, quaint and unassuming. In the words of President Reagan's daughter Maureen, "The ranch was my father's refuge, his sanctuary; it fed his soul."

Of all the possible memories, guess what my favorite part of the tour was? President Reagan's family room chair! At the time, I couldn't even tell you why. But for some reason, that chair made an enduring mental impression. I had no idea that a few years later, I would be drawn to yet another chair.

Poured In and Poured Out

After he died, I had the honor of touring one of Bob Buford's respites when he was alive—his tranquil country ranch. On weekends, Bob would often call me from there to talk about a new idea: "I need you to help me think my confusion out loud!" he would say.

Bob was always thinking about and driven to discover the next big thing God was up to in the Church. He was a multiplication thinker. His love language was anything with increasing results or potential. As long as it involved transformed lives with multiplication potential for expanding God's Kingdom, Bob was easily excited.

Throughout his life, he maintained a disciplined life rhythm. He called it his weekly "poured in" and "poured out" balance. Each week, he would spend three-and-a-half days at his ranch intentionally focused on "words, ideas, rest, and silence." He called this his time for "being poured into." Then he'd return to his home in Dallas and spend the same amount of time energized by "pouring out and into" people, work and projects. Bob contended that it's in the context of disciplined rhythms we do our best thinking.

So, I was eager to see this birthplace of so many Kingdom ideas. Bob's long-time assistant B.J. Engle showed me around, pointing out his favorite things and explaining daily rhythms on the ranch.

We both momentarily wondered why Bob, at age 78, hadn't just settled down and retired at the ranch. Why not 100 percent rest? But we both knew the answer. Bob found no biblical precedence for retirement as a principle or biblical truth. He'd say something like, "Retirement is a manmade concept. I want to finish well, and God willing, I will work productively until my last breath."

The Thinking Chair

As we continued our tour, B.J. pointed at a chair.

"That was Bob's favorite chair, where he did his best thinking and writing," she shared.

I immediately started clicking pictures. Of all the beautiful things at the ranch, once again I was drawn to an old chair. But this time, it made sense to me. The thing that captivated me about Ronald Reagan's chair is the same thing that grabbed my heart with Bob's chair. No, there isn't anything mystical about these chairs, and I don't have some weird condition that irrationally draws me to chairs.

What I do have is a passion for ideas and opportunities and strategies that can lead to 100x their impact. And I do understand that ideas lead to opportunities and opportunities to well-laid plans and well-laid plans to action and action to results. But this entire, interdependent chain starts with—and is dependent on—creating the space and rhythm for reflective thinking.

Take away the reflective thinking, and we stunt the potential for results. Reflective thinking is seed planting for a future harvest. This type of thinking then shapes the size of the fields from which we see the harvest.

I realized that this is exactly what Bob would do from that old chair at the ranch. In 1989, Peter Drucker wrote to Bob, saying, "You are very unique. Most action-oriented people don't devote so much time to thought." It's easy to be inspired by the impact of men like Peter Drucker and Bob Buford, but we can't miss the truth that great results start with disciplined rhythms for thinking.

But simply creating the space and having your thinking "chair" is not enough.

The truth is that the size of the results we often get correspond to the size of the initial dream or thinking we experience. The truth is we can't just think randomly; we must dream big! We must create a culture and discipline of multiplication thinking—learning to see the Kingdom through the lens of abundance and not scarcity. Of opportunity and not problems.

Surrendering Your Scorecard

Unfortunately, creating rhythm and space to enable multiplication thinking, and dreaming big won't really get us anywhere. If we don't have the right Kingdom-focused scorecards and motives, we won't experience the fruit of even the best multiplication thinking.

Bob was adamant about measuring results. When he turned 73, he shared with me his accounting of his life in six key areas: marriage, work, personal rhythms/disciplines, his legacy trajectory, (Leadership Network and Halftime), children and his finances. He maintained the discipline of regular personal assessments and reflections. Three years later at age 76, he shared an update to his scorecard with me. His conclusions give us an example of a surrendered scorecard.

Bob Buford's Reflections on Life at age 76

Top 3 observations/conclusions:

1. "I'm not independent anymore. It is no longer 'I'; it's now 'we.'"
2. "I could have a nice retirement, but I'm not suited for that."
3. "I'm feeling spry, but this is not the season for starting or running things. I need to be in an encourager role. I need to be doing for others what Peter Drucker did for me."

Top 3 Questions:

1. *What's the next big thing waiting to happen?*
2. *How do we get the most Kingdom impact if something happens to us? How do you put your legacy to work for 100x leverage?*
3. *How do we keep score in this next season?*

Do you see the multiplication thinking? How about the hero maker bias?

Head, Heart and Hands

Becoming a hero maker involves our head, our heart, and our hands. We must first allow Jesus to transform our thinking (head) and our motives (heart); then we'll see the work of our actions (hands) producing fruitful impact. Let's look at each one and how they fit together:

Head

Our thinking is a great place to start. Our actions (what we do with the labor of our hands) will simply be an overflow of what is in our head and our hearts. Abundant 100x results with our hands start with abundance or multiplication thinking in our minds. This is why multiplication thinking is the first essential practice of hero making. Thinking becomes the compass for directing our steps (actions). If you think accumulation, growth, and addition, don't expect to get exponential multiplying results. If you want multiplying results, start with multiplication thinking.

Heart

Armed with multiplication thinking, our motives for action must then be rightfully rooted in making and multiplying disciples (the second hero maker practice), and in seeing transformed lives. Having the right motives is a heart issue. Are we convicted by the urgency and truth that Hell is real, Heaven is now, and lost people matter to God? We must be cautious of any multiplication thinking that's rooted in things other than Kingdom-centered motives to reach lost people and make disciple makers.

Hands

The other three essential practices of hero making are issues of the hands or what we do in response to our multiplication thinking and multiplication motives. Permission giving, Gift activating, and Kingdom building are the focus of how we invest in others to help them become hero makers.

A Simple Tool for Multiplication Thinking: Dream Napkin[7]

In *Exponential: How You and Your Friends Can Start a Missional Church Movement,*[8] my brother Jon and I (Dave) tell the story of the dream God gave us and a handful of others that became Community Christian Church. The first time I ever wrote it out was on a napkin in a restaurant. I now have it in my journal, and I carry it everywhere I go, praying often as I notice it in there. I call it my dream napkin, and I've encouraged thousands of people to use the same simple tool.

Let me walk you through what to do.

1. *Napkin.* Get a paper napkin. It can be any napkin. Of course, there is nothing special about the napkin. What is special is what's about to happen between you and God.
2. *Pray and write.* Now begin to scratch out the unique dream that God might have for you—the ministry you serve, join, or create. Use symbols, words, graphics, numbers, a map, or something else.
3. *Expand by 100x.* Next, multiply your dream by one hundred—or more. This 100x vision is the Kingdom-size dream only God can do through you working through others as a hero maker.
4. *Pray and believe.* Using all the faith you have to visualize the dream on that napkin becoming reality, ask God, "How can You use me to do this?" Share your desire with God in prayer.

Do this over and over again. That's the first step toward an ongoing multiplication mindset.

In the next chapter, we'll look at what it means to give permission to others and lead with "yes." But before you move on to Hero Making Practice #2, think about and answer the "Making It Personal" reflection questions.

Making It Personal

- *Do you have a healthy "poured in" and "poured out" disciplined rhythm that enhances your ability to hear the voice of the Holy Spirit?*
- *Are you creating the space and rhythm for reflective thinking? If so, how? If not, what steps could you take to get there?*
- *Has there been a time in your life (maybe it's now) that you thought everything needed to happen through you? If so, how did you realize you were limiting yourself, people around you and ultimately, God?*
- *What big multiplication dream are you thinking about right now? The dream you and your church can't awaken on your own?*

CHAPTER 5

HeroMaker Practice 2: Permission Giving

"I'm the catapult, not the plane."

~Bob Buford

Back in junior high, I (Dave) had what I call my first "I-C-N-U" conversation.

I was at a summer camp in Indiana, and Dennis Gamauf was there. If you aren't into basketball, you probably don't know he is. But I did. Back then, I lived and died basketball, and I knew that Dennis had played in the Big 10 Conference for Purdue. All week, I was just in awe of this guy.

I remember one day we were leaving the softball field and suddenly, I just felt this big hand on my shoulder. I turned around, and it was Dennis. He said a few things about basketball and then he said, "Dave, I see in you someone who could be a really good leader."

I remember thinking, *Wow! Dennis Gamauf sees that in me?*

It happened years ago, and yet I still remember that "I-C-N-U" conversation. Dennis gave me permission to see something in me I hadn't seen.

Seeing Leadership Potential in Others

That's what the second practice in moving from hero to hero maker is all about. You begin to take the focus off your leadership and begin to see all the leadership potential God has put around you. I see what God can do through my own leadership shifts so I see what God can do through others, and I let them know what I see in them. It's a shift in *seeing*: "I see this gift in you," and "I see God at work in you when you . . ."

We find the same permission-giving throughout the life of Jesus.

When Jesus says to a group of ragtag working-class fishermen, "Come, follow me … and I will send you out to fish for people" (Matt. 4:19), He basically tells them, "I see in you what you don't see in yourselves." Here's this rabbi saying, "I think you could be a really good leader." They never expected a rabbi to see them worth teaching and leading. But Jesus saw in them a group that could change the world.

Think about what He did with Peter: "Hey Rock, on you I'm going to build my church. This movement of love is going to start with you."

And then, ultimately, He gives *us* permission, saying, "My Spirit is going to come, and you're going to be My witnesses to the ends of the earth" (Acts 1:8). Essentially, He says to us, "I see in you the potential for leading a movement that will bring My people to Me both on earth and in paradise."

Leading With 'Yes'

When you start to see the potential in the people around you, you begin to lead with a "yes" and give them permission to fully engage in the mission. The one thing every hero maker possesses that everyone around him or her needs is permission, which needs to come in the form of a "yes."

A recent study called "Growing Young"[9] reported that the more you give millennials permission—handing them the keys of everything from the church facility to the soda machine by the youth room —the more they'll thrive.

If you want to multiply leaders who, in turn, multiply leaders, you must lead with a "yes." If the people around you cannot get a "yes," they will never discover the dream God has for their lives or reach their redemptive potential. If your followers can't get permission from you with a "yes," they will never be engaged in the mission.

Six Levels for Giving Permission

Admittedly, saying yes, especially at first, is hard. There are all sorts of fears that keep us from leading with a bias to yes (we discuss these fears thoroughly in *Hero Maker*). Below are six progressive levels to help you move toward saying yes and giving permission:

- Level 1: Watch what I do, and then let's talk about it.
- Level 2: Let's together figure out a plan.
- Level 3: Propose a plan for what I should do, and let's talk about it.
- Level 4: Let me know your plan but wait for my feedback.
- Level 5: You should handle it completely, and then let me know what you did.
- Level 6: You should handle it completely, and there is no need to report back to me.

This approach helps you start to frame ministry around the response "yes." If you are going to be a permission giver, you need to develop what we call a "yes" reflex.

Recently, in an interview for our "Hero Maker" podcast, pastor, author and former NFL player Derwin Gray joined us to talk about the influencers in his life who saw greatness in him and led with a bias to yes. Now he models that same permission giving with his church in South Carolina. Eighty to ninety percent of Transformation Church's staff was at one time part of the congregation.

"We believe in multiplication and replication within the body," Derwin says, "but you have to see that in people, say it, encourage it, and then equip them for what God wants to do in and through them. As a leader, you have to ask: 'How do I give people permission to dream and then pursue that dream?'"

Five Benefits of Permission Giving

Looking back on my life, I (Todd) see the ongoing work of God as He uses just the right people, at just the right time, in just the right place, to speak just the right words of life-giving permission.

I've come to understand that the practice of permission giving is the pivotal one (out of all five) in leveraging the full potential of the other four hero-maker practices. Using permission giving to bless other people with an example of each practice offers five key benefits:

1. Permission giving casts vision. It was nearly 20 years ago for me. I was living the dream at one of the top engineering organizations in the world. I had been promoted rapidly, was making great money, loved what I was doing, yet I found myself asking pesky questions about the future.

That's when I read *Halftime: Moving from Success to Significance*[10] by Bob Buford. I didn't know Bob then, but the idea he presented—that worldly success would never fill my longing for eternal significance—resonated with my soul and contributed to my restless discontent.

Bob's words gave me permission before I knew how desperately I needed it. He could see something inside of me before I could see it myself because he had walked ahead of me. That's what permission givers do. They see what we don't see (or they see it before we do), and their simple words of encouragement serve as a catalyst to help us overcome the persistent inertia in our lives.

2. Permission giving validates personal calling. When musician Elton John reflected on reaching the milestone of 50 years in music, he said this about the importance of validation:

"George Harrison sent me a telegram, Neil Diamond introduced me on the first night at the Troubadour Club. People were extremely kind to me, and told me, and that was a validation of my work. And I think when young people have talent, I love to phone them up and say, 'Come on, well done!'"

3. Permission giving encourages action. Walt Wilson worked closely with Steve Jobs in the start-up phase at Apple, helping the company grow to $5 billion in revenue. Wilson had a successful career in Silicon Valley before shifting his focus from success to significance and founding Global Media Outreach. Bob Buford played a key role in his journey.

Several years ago, I interviewed him to ask him how Bob Buford had impacted him. Here's what he said:

> *"I was at the pinnacle of success, but I was drawn to issues of significance. I'd keep walking up to the edge of the success to significance cliff, looking over the edge, and seeing a deep dark canyon. I kept repeating the process wanting to take the step, but I never could. I read Bob's book and decided to ask for an appointment. I met with Bob for thirty minutes. He listened patiently. He stood up from his desk and walked to the white board. He drew something and said, 'Walt, if I could do this, you can do it!' That was all I needed to hear. Bob spoke permission and encouragement into my life. It's what was needed to move me to action."*

4. Permission giving builds healthy self-confidence. I never wanted to write a book. When I felt called several years ago to write a book on personal calling, I lacked confidence. I sought out best-selling author Os Guinness who had already written one of the best books I could find on calling. He provided invaluable insights, but it was his willingness to encourage me that provided the confidence I needed.

5. Permission giving multiplies impact. In a letter Bob sent to his friends about my book, *More,*[11] he said: *"I was blessed to have Peter Drucker, the father of modern management, as my personal mentor and friend. He helped me discern and refine my personal calling. He challenged me with three questions:*

- *Who am I? (a question of **being** or design)*
- *What am I to contribute? (a question of **doing** or mission)*
- *Where can I be most useful? (a question of **going** or position)*

"Unfortunately, most people never discover or engage their unique personal calling. They get stuck in the patterns of the past while dreaming of a more meaningful future. Their unique gifts and strengths lie dormant like a treasure that is never found hidden in a mattress. Imagine the impact of mobilizing a movement of Christians, living out their God-given calling!"

Are You a Permission Giver?

Are you best known as a permission giver, a role recruiter, or a self-reliant doer?

- **Permission givers** let others know what they see in them. In seeing the potential in others, permission givers say it, encourage it, and then equip others for what God wants to do in and through them.
- **Role recruiters** mobilize people to fill the most pressing needs of the organization. They naturally see the gifts of people as critical resources for growing the local organization and overcoming its current barriers and obstacles.
- **Self-reliant doers** are critical to the operation of the organization and tend to be lone rangers who spend most of their time doing the things they perceive only they can do. They are so busy balancing their primary responsibilities that they find little time for directly investing in the development of others to take some of their workload.

Which of the following do others hear you say most often?

- "I see in you…" (permission giver)
- "I need you to…" (role recruiter)
- "I will do it…" (self-reliant doer)

A Simple Tool for Giving Permission: I-C-N-U Conversation[12]

An effective tool we believe in wholeheartedly is simply a conversation—one person calling out greatness in another person. It's a simple formula that helps create a "yes" environment. All you do is say, "I see [blank] in you." You fill in the blank with the appropriate affirmation.

We call ICNU the four most important letters of the alphabet. We encourage everyone—you don't have to serve in any official capacity—to regularly tell others, "I see this ability in you," "I see this gift in you," and "I see God at work in you when you . . ."

As you learn to invest in and give permission to others and see the impact it makes, Scripture promises us that we will bear fruit. This is what we're talking about when we think of the third practice in hero making: multiplying disciples. Take a few minutes to think through the questions below and then read on to unpack the most critical of all five hero-making practices.

Making It Personal

- *Who gave you permission and modeled what it means and looks like to be a permission giver?*
- *Why do you think permission giving is so integral to becoming a hero maker? Why are not running everything and not leading everything so critical to being effective hero makers who push others into the spotlight?*
- *Was there ever a time in your life or ministry that you sensed you were leading with "no"? What did that look like?*

- *How did you realize you were leading with no? What impact did it have on others, especially those you were developing as leaders?*
- *Are there certain indicators, maybe even red flags, you've developed for yourself and your team that indicate how well you and they are doing at being permission givers?*
- *What practical steps can you put in place to lead and facilitate the permission-giving process and leading with yes?*

CHAPTER 6

HeroMaker Practice 3: Disciple Multiplying

"There is more to giving than feeling good. The joy is found in the results of transformed lives."

~Bob Buford

When you think about Jesus' ministry, do you imagine Him spending most of His time preaching sermons to crowds, feeding and healing people wherever He went? Or do you think of Him as spending time with the twelve men He selected and taught?

When I (Dave) set out to write *Hero Maker*, I and my co-author, Warren Bird, researched the Gospels to get a real, up-close look at how Jesus spent His time. Our research revealed that three-fourths of Jesus' time on earth was spent training the twelve disciples. From the time He told them to go out and multiply in Matthew 4:19 to His death, 73 percent of His time was with the Twelve. The Gospels record forty-six events spent with the disciples compared to seventeen events with the masses—almost three to one.

We can learn from this, and I hope we do. There's an easily overlooked verse in John 3:22 that says, "After this, Jesus and his disciples went out into the Judean countryside, where He *spent some time with them*." The

Greek word for "spend time with" is this composite word, *diatribo. Dia* means "against"; and *tribo* means "to rub." So *diatribo* literally means "to spend time together rubbing off on each other."

The point of Jesus' ministry—why He spent three-fourths of His time with the few—was that they would do greater things. That was the goal. He knew the mission would be accomplished through them and the people they would disciple who would disciple others and so on. And the way to do this was just spending time together, rubbing off on them.

With His life, Jesus showed us how to multiply disciples—the third practice in hero making.

A Modern-Day Disciple Multiplier

Here's the difference between heroes and hero makers. Heroes share what they know; hero makers share their lives. Hero makers invest in the development of leaders who invest in the development of leaders to the fourth generation.

The difference is subtle but big.

When you're committed to this third practice of being a disciple multiplier, the impact reaches beyond your church and your city. My friend and former apprentice (and leader who led Todd to know Jesus), Troy McMahon, is a great example. Troy worked at General Mills and did a great job as an apprentice in my small group. In fact, he soon became the leader of it, and I went on to start another group. As Troy continued to lead, we asked him to be a coach for our small group leaders. Eventually, he wound up joining our staff and became our first campus pastor.

Eleven years ago, Troy planted Restoration Church in Kansas City with NewThing, our church-planting network. Today in 2018, Restore now has more than one thousand people at three locations and has helped plant more than forty churches. On top of that, Troy's leading a network of church-planting churches in Kansas City!

"Our dream is to invest in others and to see 100 churches planted in the city in the next 10 years," Troy says.

Troy has a goal in mind: "If we can embed the reproductive DNA in those churches, then by the end of that decade we'll see a number of those churches reproduce," he told me. "And so, it's not just starting the first generation; we're starting the second or third generation as well."

This is the kind of disciple multiplying that advances Exponential's "4-10 mission"—to see the number of Level 4 reproducing U.S. churches increase from four percent to greater than ten percent. When we see disciple multipliers who birth new communities of faith, we will begin to move the needle to a transformative tipping point.

We've Got to Get This Right

This third hero-making practice is simultaneously the most crucial and the most difficult one to execute. Both Todd and I are convinced that we've got to get this one right because when we get this one right, all of the other practices fall into place. Todd likens it to the rudder that controls the ship's path. Disciple multiplying gives direction to the hero maker's journey, he says. Without it, our efforts might produce good fruit while actually missing the target Jesus is calling us to.

I'll let him explain.

Like Dave says, multiplying disciples the way Jesus did is critical to hero making and multiplication. That's why Jesus spent so much of His time doing it and why He verbally and pointedly called us to make disciples.

Think about it. When you want your team to do something, you look for the simplest, clearest way to communicate your goal, right? When my wife wants me to fix something in the house, she doesn't mince words. I know what she is "calling" me to do.

Jesus didn't mince words either. When I read Scripture, I see no wiggle room in the fact that Jesus commanded us to make and multiply disciples. He was crystal clear! It's not intended to be complex. In the simplicity of His strategy, Jesus knows that if we focus on making disciples the way He did, we will see Kingdom multiplication. If we cooperate with Him in this simple strategy, the Holy Spirit will produce the harvest.

The core of any multiplication movement is disciple making. It is the first and critical dimension of Kingdom multiplication. The question is simple: *Are you focused on producing biblical disciples who make disciples that plant churches that plant churches as your primary motive and cause?*

Unfortunately, we don't always hear and embrace the simplicity of Jesus' command. Instead of focusing on disciple making as our core purpose that drives all of our programming, we tend to align our activities around other motives (one of the three shifts I talked about in chapter 2). With the wrong motives, we find ourselves pursuing the path of the hero rather than the hero maker.

Without disciple making that multiplies and produces new communities of faith, we have little hope of moving the multiplication needle. And we'll fall desperately short of Jesus' call. When we don't see new disciple-making churches birthed, we limit our future capacity for disciple making.

Jesus, An Activist for _____

Dave talked about Jesus' actions. Now let's look at Jesus' words. I challenge you to read all of the red-letter words in the four Gospels, focusing on what I call Jesus' activism. Activists vigorously advocate for a cause or issue. Their passion gives voice to their heart. An activist's cause gives them reason to get out of bed in the morning and to lie awake at night. Some are blessed with thoughtfully pursuing the thing they want to be remembered for!

Using that definition, look at Jesus' words. What do you find? If you were writing His epitaph—"Jesus, an activist for [fill in the blank]"—what word would you fill in? Be careful not to single out individual verses that support your particular cause. Instead, look for the underlying thread that runs throughout His ministry.

Let's start with what would *not* be on the list. Let me make it personal. I'm an activist for church planting and multiplication. I'm willing to give the rest of my life to seeing the percentage of U.S. churches that ever reproduce increase from less than 4 percent to greater than 10 percent. Because of that, I'd sure like for Jesus' epitaph to end with "church planting and multiplication." I often act as if it does.

But no matter how passionate I am about my cause, Jesus was not primarily an activist for church planting and multiplication. Yes, He cares about it, but He knows that if we focus on making healthy biblical disciples, we'll get church planting and multiplication as one byproduct of the fruit.

It's sobering to realize that if I elevate my cause to be above His—even if my cause is multiplying His Church—I'm practicing a form of idolatry.

Jesus gave us a clear, compelling and primary cause—intended to tie together all of our other worldly efforts for good: Jesus, an activist for disciple making! The kind built around the full surrender to his Lordship. The *diatribo* kind that looks different than the world, and in its full maturity, has no choice but to multiply and result in people mobilized to make a difference in the injustices in the world.

Puritan Minister Cotton Mather used a great metaphor to describe the consequences of elevating our secondary callings (including our activist pursuits) above our primary calling to be disciples who make disciples. Mather describes a rowboat propelled by two oars. One oar represents our primary calling (to be disciple makers and multipliers) and the other oar our secondary calling. Put no oars in the water and you drift with the winds of culture. Put only one oar in the water, and you spin in circles.

When our activist causes take priority over our primary calling to multiply disciples, it's like having only one oar in the water. No matter how loud we trumpet the message of our cause, we just spin in circles. Only when we put both oars in the water do we make forward progress.

Keeping the Main Thing the Main Thing

As a community, let's commit to keeping Jesus' main thing our main thing. Let's leverage our unique gifts and calling to be activists for good. But let's also position our activism so that our primary fruits produce a movement of biblical disciple multipliers. In doing so, we'll unleash a movement of love and transformation on the world!

Heroes add while hero makers multiply. Heroes are remembered for *what* they did, while hero makers are remembered for *who* they invested in.

So, which is it for you? Hero or hero maker? What or who? Addition or multiplication?

If you want to be a hero maker, you must first embrace and then keep the main thing the main thing. The first two essential practices of hero making—multiplication thinking and permission giving—are important. But, the third essential practice, disciple multiplying, gives us the motive and mission for doing what we do.

A Simple Tool for Disciple Multiplying: Five Steps to Apprenticeship[13]

This tool for disciple multiplication has the potential to exponentially increase the impact of your leadership. Before you use this tool, pull out your dream napkin I (Dave) gave you in chapter 1 for multiplication thinking. Now ask, "Who are the specific people and leaders I want to develop so that my dream napkin can become true someday?" Your next step is to take some of them through the five steps of apprenticeship.

1. I do. You watch. We talk. This includes asking the following questions: "What worked?" "What didn't work?" and "How can we

54

improve?" This time of debriefing needs to continue throughout the five steps.

2. I do. You help. We talk. In this step of development, you give your apprentice an opportunity to help lead part of the small group meeting: "Could you lead the icebreaker time at the beginning if I lead the rest?" Again, the small group meeting should be followed up with a one-on-one debrief between leader and apprentice.

3. You do. I help. We talk. Now your apprentice transitions from helping you to taking on most of the leadership responsibilities for the small group: "Could you lead most of the meeting this week? If you do, I will handle the icebreaker at the beginning and the prayer time at the end, plus I will be there with you the whole time." You are gradually releasing responsibilities to his new, developing leader.

4. You do. I watch. We talk. The apprentice process is almost complete as your apprentice grows increasingly more confident in their role as a leader. You have him lead the entire meeting each week while you watch him, and you give him the responsibility of finding a service project for the group. At your debrief time, you say, "I think you are ready for leadership; do you think you are ready?" With both leader and apprentice feeling ready for the next step, you both begin to plan. Will he take over the group or lead a new group, and you will lead next.

5. You do. Someone else watches. This is where the process of multiplication comes full circle. You say to your apprentice, "You have done great! Have you started to think about who you can mentor and repeat this process with?" Your former apprentice is now leading and begins developing new apprentices. Since you have developed and released several apprentices, you continue to work with him and other leaders in a coaching capacity.

The third practice of disciple multiplying dovetails into the fourth practice of hero making: gift activating. When we multiply disciples the way Jesus did, we start to see their gifts and talents like Jesus saw the Twelve's and sent them out to do what He had modeled and taught them to do through His actions and words—a revolution that would change the world.

Making It Personal

- *Did it surprise you to learn that Jesus spent three-fourths of His ministry modeling discipleship with the small group of twelve? Why or why not?*
- *Who are you diatriboing with? Who is rubbing off on you these days, and who are you rubbing off on?*
- *Are you sharing more of what you know or are you sharing your life? How are you investing in the development of leaders who invest in the development of leaders to the fourth generation? If so, how? If not, why not?*
- *Why do you think multiplying disciples is the most critical of all the five practices of a hero maker? Why do we have to get this right?*
- *What can you do in your life and ministry to keep the main thing the main thing? List at least three actions below.*

CHAPTER 7

HeroMaker Practice 4: Gift Activating

"We are called to be the platform, not the show."

~Bob Buford

I (Dave) will never forget being at Nairobi Chapel in Kenya and seeing the senior pastor and my friend Oscar Muriu invite thirty-one men and women to join him on stage. These people had just gone through the third and final track of their Kinara Leadership Program to learn what it means to be a multiplying church.

Oscar went on to explain that the church was commissioning all thirty-one of these leaders to go and plant new churches in Kibera, the largest slum in Africa. He looked at the graduates, affirming his belief in their gifts and ability. Then he looked at the congregation and asked them to join him in praying for them. As he prayed, he reached out his hand toward the new leaders as a sign of blessing and asked the congregation to do the same. I've never seen that many church planters commissioned by one church on one Sunday!

Pastor Oscar is a hero maker who understands the importance of gift activating.

The fourth hero maker practice we have identified is gift activating—a shift in blessing. Instead of asking God to bless the use of our own gifts, we learn to ask God to bless leaders we're sending out. Gift activating requires that we not fill slots but instead develop people's gifts and commission leaders to be sent out for ministry.

We can see the most obvious example of gift activating in the life of Jesus, specifically in Matthew 28. He has been walking with these men He selected, living life with them and modeling disciple making, and now He's going to turn over the movement to His closest followers. He tells them, "I have all authority, and now I'm going to use it through you as you go out." With that, He literally commissions them to go into the world and make disciples, and He activates their gifts.

As hero makers, we need to find those kinds of moments for the people leaders we're multiplying.

The Key Moment in Gift Activation

The Underground Network in Tampa, Florida, is another great example of gift activating. The Underground is a family of microchurches. Each of these microchurches starts with one question they ask people to answer: "What would you do if you were not afraid?"

They take the answers to that question and then build communities around that mission to reach people who aren't directly encountering the gospel. They wait a year to commission these leaders to see if the idea gets traction and make sure leaders are committed. Then they lay hands on them, bless them and send them out.

I hope God gives you opportunities to commission and send out thirty-one church planters. But I think the key moment is this gift activation or commissioning. In its simplest form, commissioning is the process of blessing a person or team and affirming the use of the gifts God has given them.

Commissioning can be done for a leader (or leadership team) starting a new group or team. It can be done for an individual (or a team) starting a new church. I (Dave) have commissioned new small group leaders in a home, people who are leaving to start a new ministry or church at staff meetings in restaurants.

Exponential Moments of Gift Activating

At the Exponential conference, the last session is always a gift-activating moment. Over the past ten years, we have commissioned thousands of people. Personally, it's fun for me to look back over my shoulder at some of these moments. Some of the most impactful churches in the country have in some ways come to life at that moment.

Ryan Kwon was sitting in the middle balcony when he decided to go forward. Recently, we talked to him and he shared his powerful story, I'll let him share how it unfolded in his own words:

"At the last session, I was sitting in the same seat up in the balcony, removed enough to not be pulled into the things but at the same time all there. I was taking some notes, and Francis Chan comes up. I'll never forget that he gave us an invitation to come up and be prayed for if we were considering planting. To be honest, I wasn't considering planting at the time. I was thinking about it. I'd been challenged by it. But I wasn't feeling called to it.

"Then Francis started introducing a song that we were going to sing together called 'Consuming Fire,' and he said, 'I love this song because it starts out by saying, 'There must be more than this.' 'Do you ever feel that way?' he asked the crowd.

"And I remember thinking, *That's me. I feel like that all the time.* What really impacted me was when he said, 'If you're scared to plant a church, I want you to know it's okay. And that's why we want to pray for you.'

"It was the first time that I realized why I didn't want to plant a church: I was scared. I was scared of failure. I was scared that the calling to plant a church was a call to success and to build a big church and to disciple a lot of people and I thought to myself, *I don't need or want that pressure. I'm just scared.*

"But the gospel addressed me that day. The gospel doesn't call us to success. It calls us to faithfulness. And I felt that in my heart. So, I had to stand. And I remember turning to my friend who came with me and saying, 'I'm jumping. I'm going for it.'

"I made that long walk down the long stairway all the way up to the front, and I knelt down and surrendered all of my fears to God. I just knew that God was talking to me, and I just knew that God was calling me to plant a church."

Since then, Ryan has planted Resonate Church in Fremont, California, which now has two campuses, and is planting another church. That day, Ryan's gift of apostolic leadership was activated.

We've changed a lot of the things we do at the Exponential conference, but one of the things we've never changed (and never will) is the commissioning service where we facilitate these transformational gift-activating moments that lead to new communities of faith.

That's what hero makers do.

Are You Just Filling Slots?

My (Todd) guess is that every leader knows what that somewhat cryptic question means when it comes to mobilizing people's gifts and talents.

Are you taking the time to identify, develop and activate the gifts of the people in your church where they can pursue their passions and God-given calling (even if it's outside your church walls)? Or are you basically filling a need in your church with a warm body that has stepped up to volunteer?

That's what we're talking about with this idea that Dave has introduced. Essentially, we look for opportunities to activate people's unique sweet spot of personal calling and move from mobilizing people with an "I can do it, you can help" motive to a "you can do it, how can I help" open-handed posture. Bottom line: We rethink and change our definition of success from people being recruited to fill our volunteer slots to people being mobilized on their unique gifting and calling for God's purposes and impact.

That's what Bob Buford did for me and countless others. Bob was a true gift activator. He understood that he had a choice. He could celebrate the number of people who cooperated with his call for their service or he could celebrate the number of people whom he was leading to discover and engage God's unique calling for their lives—*wherever* that took them.

In the last chapters, I (Todd) talked about calling—that we have a primary calling of making disciples and a unique personal calling, which gives each of us a unique role and purpose in God's general disciple-making calling. The cool thing is that Jesus and the Holy Spirt apportion our unique gifts to us. Our role, then, is to discover and embrace the gifts they've already instilled in us as part of our unique DNA—and then help others identify and activate their gifts.

As we discover and steward our unique gifts and calling, Scripture tells us that the family of believers we call our local church are then called to *affirm and activate those gifts.* Our best example may be the early church at Antioch. In Acts 13:1-3, we read:

> *Now in the church at Antioch there were prophets and teachers: Barnabas, Simeon called Niger, Lucius of Cyrene, Manaen (who had been brought up with Herod the tetrarch) and Saul. While they were worshiping the Lord and fasting, the Holy Spirit said, "Set apart for me Barnabas and Saul for the work to which I have called them." So, after they had fasted and prayed, they placed their hands on them and sent them off.*

In these three short verses, we get a glimpse into gift activating. We see an inward discernment of calling that happens between God and these individuals ("the work to which I have called them"); and an outward affirmation of calling that's affirmed by the Holy Spirit and happens corporately.

The Inward Discernment of Calling

In my book, *More: Find Your Personal Calling and Live Life to the Fullest Measure*,[14] I (Todd) highlight three elements of all sweet spots that are found in nature. We also have a sweet spot of personal calling. These elements include a design (be), a purpose (do), and a position (go): Who am I created to *be*? What am I made to *do*? Where am I to *go*?

The discernment of our unique personal calling is about discovering our unique integration of these BE-DO-GO questions. Some specific examples:

- Paul, an apostle of Christ Jesus (BE), who plants the gospel message (and churches) (DO), among the Gentiles (GO).
- Billy Graham, an evangelist of Christ Jesus (BE), calling people to repentance (DO), in large stadiums in strategic cities (GO).
- Mother Teresa, a shepherd of Christ Jesus (BE), caring for downcast and needy people (DO), in poverty-stricken areas (GO).
- Martin Luther King, a prophet of Christ Jesus (BE), calling for racial equality and reconciliation (DO), in the United States (GO).

Our human nature is to want clarity on all three elements before acting. For two full years, I wrestled with God, begging for clarity about my vocation and profession. I had pretty good clarity on my BE but kept getting stuck on the DO. In hindsight, I realize that God wanted my full surrender and willingness to GO as a prerequisite to eventually give me clarity on the DO.

What if your top stewardship role is to activate the gifts of people to GO so that they can more fully discover and engage their unique sweet spot of calling? What if the biggest barrier to mobilizing an army of everyday missionaries to unique mission fields in every crack and corner of society is *us*?

They're difficult questions. But they are questions we need to honestly think about and urgently ask.

When we seek to define the GO for other people in an attempt to fill slots and advance our priorities, *we potentially become a barrier standing in the way of them living the life God meant for them.* The outcome of these missteps makes ripples throughout eternity. To hear the words "Well done good and faithful steward," *we must see the unique gifts of the people we lead as precious resources ordained by God.*

The Outward Affirmation of Calling

Going back to Acts 13, we see great wisdom from the example of Paul and Barnabas being set apart and sent from the church in Antioch. There are no prescriptive criteria, but in these three verses, we do see five noteworthy characteristics at work:

1. *"In the church"* – The spiritual authority for setting apart, activating, and sending leaders was found within the local church. The local body in Antioch did not need to get permission from Jerusalem, or some external governing body. The local leaders, in the local church, had the authority to affirm and send.
2. *Guidance of the Holy Spirit* – The local body took seriously the importance of "setting apart" leaders and activating their gifts. Those in spiritual authority sought the guidance, wisdom, and leading of the Holy Spirit.
3. *Affirmation of calling* – Paul and Barnabas had discerned their calling from the Lord. The local church in Antioch then affirmed that calling by publicly setting them apart.
4. *Prayer and fasting* – We know the importance of prayer and fasting, but how often do we just give it lip service? My close friend Bobby

Harrington and co-founder of Discipleship.org is a student of discipline-making movements. In nearly every planning meeting we have for future initiatives, Bobby reminds us of the vital and critical practice of prayer and fasting as a foundation for gift activation.

5. *Laying on of hands*– While this is often a sign of imparting the Holy Spirit, this context in Antioch is like a visible, public sign of commissioning and sending. A celebration of sorts.

Five Important Reasons for Gift Activating and Public Commissioning

Earlier in this chapter, Dave introduced the concept of commissioning others. I (Todd) want to conclude by looking at some specific reasons for commissioning and how it is such an integral part of gift activating.

Let's look again at Acts 13 and role play for a minute.

Imagine being in the church in Antioch, but you don't have the benefit of knowing the outcome of Paul's and Barnabas' missionary journey. You're part of the team praying and fasting for Paul and Barnabas. You see the process of the local leaders seeking the guidance of the Holy Spirit, and then you see their prayers answered. You attend the public commissioning where the entire assembly lays on hands, gives them words of encouragement, cries with them (they knew they would likely not see them again this side of Heaven), and sends them off with hugs of affirmation.

You know that you're part of something bigger than yourself. You anticipate hearing amazing stories upon their return (hopefully) or in Paradise. Down deep, you know they are doing something really significant, and you feel blessed to play a small role in their story. You even find yourself wondering if there is a similar adventure for you!

Now, put yourself in Paul's and Barnabas' shoes. You *are not* heading out on a cushy, all-expenses paid vacation to a sunny Caribbean getaway. You know the journey has no certainty of return and may likely be the most difficult thing you've ever done. You're not sure where you're going, when (or whether) you will return, what will happen to you, and how you will fund your journey. Persecution is likely. But, you have a clear calling and the spiritual affirmation of your local church family.

How important is the affirmation of your sending church? How critical are their prayers and public words of encouragement? The experience was one Paul and Barnabas would cherish throughout their journey. It would be life-sustaining.

Using what I have come to see as an extremely moving and powerful story in Scripture, we can identify at least five key benefits of a public commissioning or "setting apart" for gift activating. They are benefits we can experience in our local churches.

1. *Affirmation of calling*– Imagine growing up and never hearing your parents affirm what you're good at (I realize this may be reality for many of you who are reading this). A single sentence of affirmation can change the trajectory of a person's life. The church has the ability to play a special role that no one else can play in activating the gifts of its members.

2. *Blessing and permission to GO*–In our time together, Bob often said to me, "Everyone needs permission and encouragement to be who God made them to be." In our zeal to put people into slots to grow our local thing, we can unintentionally stifle the GO. People need to receive our blessing and permission to GO.

3. *Encouragement for the journey*– Living out our calling, especially when it's in the unfriendly cracks and crannies of society beyond the safe walls of the church, requires encouragement. When we celebrate major milestones in life, we are thanking God for what He has done in the past while simultaneously drawing encouragement for the road ahead.

4. *Unifying a home base of support*– When we see our mission field as the cracks and crannies beyond the safe walls of the church, a home base of support is vital (just like it was for Paul and Barnabas). We need

the prayers and ongoing encouragement of others. We need to know we are not alone on our journey.

5. *Inspire and challenge others to GO* – Gift activating is contagious. When people see others taking great steps of faith and surrender for God, they are also drawn into the story. *They begin to see their own story as part of the narrative of God's bigger story.* Our public commissioning efforts are uniquely positioned to inspire and draw others into the journey.

A Simple Tool for Gift Activating: Commissioning[15]

Commissioning is the simple process of blessing a person or team and affirming the use of the gifts God has given them. It will most likely involve two components:

1. Laying your hands on them as a sign of affirmation.
2. Praying for God to bless them as you send them out.

Commissioning can be done for a leader (or leadership team) starting a new group or team. It can be done for an individual (or a team) starting a new church. The commissioning is an important relational and personal blessing that hero makers give to those they are developing.

That's why at every Exponential live event, we always end with a commissioning service. It's our favorite time of the event—when God's people actually step forward to say "yes, I want to use my gifts for the Kingdom."

We ask leaders to take action by coming to the front of the room, and we anoint and pray for them. We consider it their ordination. (If you've never been to an Exponential commissioning service, anyone who has been would tell you you're missing out.) And if you're not doing it in your church, you're missing a huge opportunity to activate gifts for the Kingdom. Talk about a living legacy!

We've done this for many years at Community Christian, and I (Dave) am always stunned at how seriously people take this idea of being commissioned for a specific mission. Every year, I hear people say things like,

- "I don't want to merely coach my Little League team. I'm looking for opportunities to help many of those families find their way back to God."
- "We're going to adopt a child, joining many other Christian families who together dream of zeroing out our state's foster child waiting list."
- "I'm going to start a small group at work."
- "After going on three mission trips to Haiti, God's call is clear: we're going to move there, to make a difference."

Through the laying on of hands and praying a blessing on people, we convey a powerful message: if you are a Christ follower, we want to help you activate the unique gifts and calling that God has given you.

Are you ready to stop filling slots and be a gift activator? Check out the questions below and answer them with your team. Then read on to learn about the final practice in hero making—the one that brings together everything we've said over the last six chapters … and keeps us on the lifelong adventure of hero making.

Making It Personal

- *How does our approach to "setting apart" and activating gifts differ from the church at Antioch? How is it similar?*
- *What are the potential benefits of more intentionally and publicly commissioning people for ministry in our unique context and culture?*
- *What obstacles and barriers would we run into (or are running into)?*
- *What steps or decisions could we make today that would elevate the importance of gift activating within our church?*

CHAPTER 8

HeroMaker Practice 5: Kingdom Building

"We need to transform the latent energy in the pews of the Church into active energy."

~Bob Buford

If you're like most church leaders, you tend to ask, "How do I grow my church?" It's a good question—one that I (Dave) have asked many times, especially in the early years of planting Community Christian. But you probably know by now, there are better questions we could be asking.

Let me tell you why I think we need to rethink this question by looking at it in four parts:

1. **How do I…**: The third word in the question is where we need to start because I think we may have the wrong pronoun here. Nowhere in Scripture do I see anything that says we're supposed to do ministry alone. God wired us for relationship with Him and with others. We're meant to pursue His mission together, as one body. What if we said, "I want to do this through multiplying leaders." So, the first part of this question now becomes: "How do we …?"

2. **How do I *grow* ...** Growth is a good thing. Healthy things grow. We want our churches to grow. But we don't grow to create seating capacity. This is where the shift from hero to hero maker comes in. We want to grow to create sending capacity. That's a big difference. If that's the case, then maybe instead of "grow," we use the word "multiply." So, the next part becomes, "How do we *multiply* ...?"

3. **How do I grow *my* ...** As leaders, we fall into the trap of thinking this is "my church." But let's be honest. We're just stewards of God's church. It's not *our church*. Maybe we need to ax "my church" from our vocabulary because it's God's church. So, instead of, "How do I grow *my* church?" maybe we should be asking, "How do we multiply *God's* ....?"

4. **How do I grow my *church*?** Let me make a fourth correction because when we say "church," we almost always mean church with a little c—my local church. Actually, what I think we see in Matthew 6:33 ("Seek first the Kingdom of God...") is that what Jesus is really concerned about is the Kingdom. So, what if we began to ask, "How do we multiply God's *Kingdom*?

That's where the fifth and final hero maker practice comes in ... Kingdom building is a shift in counting. Instead of counting the people who show up at "my thing," you begin to count the leaders whom you send to go out and do "God's thing." The only thing that matters—that ultimately counts—is advancing the Kingdom of God. If we're really serious about becoming hero makers, we need to make a shift in the questions we ask.

Two Church Problems

You see there are two problems with the question "How do I grow my church?" The first is that it's entirely possible for church attendance to be growing, but the Kingdom of God is actually shrinking. In fact, there are more people going to church in the United States than ever before, which may make us think *we're winning*. The truth is we're not winning because a smaller percentage of the population is attending church.

It's also entirely possible for a church to be growing, but the *impact* is shrinking. A church's growing attendance does not promise that people are growing spiritually. Attendance graphs that are up and to the right don't guarantee that people are faithful in following Jesus. I believe that for Jesus, winning was measured most in expanding God's Kingdom.

Ultimately, God is concerned about transformation. If we're going to be salt and light, we have to change how we count.

The Fruit of Kingdom Building

So, what happens when this Kingdom-building shift from hero to hero maker happens? Let me (Todd) suggest that the fruit is mobilization. The outcome of leaders shifting their personal scorecards from "me" to "others" should allow us to see the mobilization of the priesthood of all believers.

We're heavy into planning our 2019 Exponential theme, "Made for More: Mobilizing God's People, God's Way." We strategically and intentionally selected this theme because we believe and have seen that the mobilization of believers is the next natural progression beyond hero making. I've come to realize the practices of hero making and Kingdom building, in particular, are inseparable from mobilization. All pathways to seeing multiplication and movements of healthy reproducing churches seem to converge on the issue of mobilizing God's people.

Let me clarify what I mean by mobilization by going back to the "primary" and "secondary" callings I've talked about in these chapters. When I refer to the practice of "mobilization of God's people, God's way," I'm referring to both of these callings. Instead of simply filling slots to grow and operate our churches, we need to deploy disciples into their unique mission fields where they work, live, study and play.

A Surprising Search Through Scripture

As we've pulled this theme together, we've wrestled with how to define believers who are being mobilized in their unique sweet spot of calling. We know we want a word or phrase that best captures all of the roles Christ has given His people as we're mobilized to carry His fullness into every corner of the world (our primary calling).

That search led me to an in-depth study of the New Testament that revealed some surprising discoveries about Kingdom building and how we should measure the impact of our efforts to be hero makers. I started out looking for "of Jesus" and "of Christ" references. When it was all said and done, I found more than 50 examples, but I also realized that all of these examples naturally fit into one of three categories or buckets:

1. What Jesus did for us as He showed His love for us!
2. How He equips us to share His love—the special equipping Jesus gives us to become more like Him and to carry His fullness to others.
3. The actions or roles He has called us to as we share His love

Let's take a closer look at all three buckets:

1. What Jesus Did for Us (a.k.a. the gospel narrative)

The following words—collected from the "of Christ Jesus" references I found—give us a succinct narrative of the gospel:

The *obedience* of Jesus and the *sinlessness* of Jesus made Him the perfect redeemer of mankind; The *persecution* of Jesus, the *sacrifice* of Jesus, and the spilled *blood* of Jesus and the *resurrection* of Jesus on the third day made possible the *eternal Kingdom* of Jesus where forgiven *disciples* of Jesus will spend eternity with Him.

2. How Jesus Equips Us

The following words—collected from the "of Christ Jesus" references—give us a comprehensive description of the numerous ways in which Jesus equips us to become more like Him and to carry His fullness to others:

In the **church** of Jesus and the **fellowship** of Jesus, the **called** of Jesus have the **presence** of Jesus and the **Spirit** of Jesus walking in the **power** of Jesus and the **authority** of Jesus as they carry the **fullness** of Jesus, the **knowledge** of Jesus, the **example** of Jesus, and the **teaching** of Jesus, while proclaiming the **freedom** of Jesus, the **holiness** of Jesus, the **grace** of Jesus, the **mercy** of Jesus and the **affection** of Jesus to a lost and dying world.

3. The Kingdom-Building Roles He Has Called Us To

Finally, the words—collected from the "of Christ Jesus" references—offer a succinct list of the roles Jesus calls us to carry. Collectively, these roles give us helpful context for considering what God's way of mobilization looks like. It also gives us the lens through which to develop and measure a Kingdom-building scorecard:

We are to be **disciples** of Jesus, **ambassadors** of Jesus, **servants** of Jesus, **ministers** of Jesus, **prisoners** of Jesus, **soldiers** of Jesus, and the **aroma** of Jesus to a lost and dying world.

Mobilizing Everyday Missionaries

Each of these words brings unique distinctives. Together, they help paint a vivid picture of godly mobilization. If I could pick just one word or phrase to capture the collective characteristics of these roles, I would pick "everyday missionary."

Mobilization is about *equipping and deploying everyday missionaries into their unique mission fields where they work, live, study and play.* And it's why Kingdom building is a helpful and important bridge to mobilization.

If you were designing a strategy for Kingdom building, what better way to do it than mobilizing an army of everyday missionaries into their unique mission fields in all corners of society? As Bob would always say, "We need to transform the latent energy in the pews of the Church into active energy."

The process of surrendering a life of success to one of significance is, in itself, a catalyst for embracing a new scorecard and a different way of measuring what's important. By dying to self and embracing new values for measuring success, we position ourselves for Kingdom building.

We do that with a Kingdom-building scorecard that helps us measure how well we're doing with mobilizing disciples over accumulation. How well are we doing with identifying the unique calling of everyday missionaries and deploying them to carry the fullness and aroma of Jesus into every nook and cranny of society?

As we honestly answer these questions and start to change what we count, we position ourselves to witness the fruit of mobilization. Ultimately, to see God's Kingdom come.

When you quit asking, "How do I grow my church," and start asking, "How do we multiply God's Kingdom?" you begin to focus on what matters to Jesus–His priority. We'll say it again because it's so important you get this. Hero makers don't just count who shows up at *my* **thing**. They count who they're sending out to do *God's* thing.

And God's thing—being more like Jesus as we lead and multiply others—is what hero making is about. We learn to identify our calling and others' callings, make the critical shifts we've defined in each chapter and play our unique role in God's unfolding story.

A Simple Tool for Kingdom Building: Your Hero Maker's Scoreboard[16]

Now it's *your* turn to develop a scoreboard that will help you focus on being a hero maker and not the hero. A winning scoreboard must show that you are faithfully building the Kingdom.

We suggest you keep track of only two measurements: first, how many apprentices you have; second, how many total apprentices you and your apprentices have developed. This is a simple scoreboard that you can easily keep on your phone, your laptop, or even a scrap of paper. Let me (Dave) explain these two Kingdom-building stats.

1. Measure Current Apprentices

Ask yourself these questions: "How many people am I investing in?" "How many people am I mentoring to be commissioned to do great things?" "How many people am I taking through the hero-making process?" Apprenticing relationships are not hard to count. Usually, leaders have only a handful of apprentices at a time. Jesus had twelve. I (Dave) doubt I've ever had that many at any one time.

If you are a small group leader and you are developing an apprentice, that is one. If you are a ministry leader and you have a team of four whom you are growing and meeting with regularly to expand their ministry, that would be four. If you are a lead pastor and you have an apprentice in your small group, a leadership resident who is going on to plant a church, and your executive staff team of five whom you hope grow beyond you, that would be a total of seven.

This is intentionally simple but ultimately important.

2. Measure Cumulative Apprentices

The second measurement on a hero maker's scoreboard is the total number of apprentices that you and your apprentices have ever developed and released. The most proficient of hero makers have a hard time keeping track of this second measurement. That should be your goal—you develop so many leaders who develop so many leaders who develop so many leaders that you have lost count after the fourth generation.

However, until you get past the fourth generation, we encourage you to keep track.

We started this book asking, "Are you a hero or a hero maker?" We hope by now you're not only thinking about it but that you're on the path to becoming one and as hero maker Bob Buford reminds us, intent on seeing your fruit grow on others' trees.

Making It Personal

- *Are you asking, "How do I grow my church?" or "How do we multiply God's Kingdom?" What's your focus? What would others say is your focus?*
- *Was there ever a time in your life or ministry that you sensed you were counting and measuring the wrong things?*
- *If so, how did you realize that?*
- *After reading this book, are you ready to invest in apprentices?*
- *Do you agree with the statement: "It is entirely possible for a church's attendance to be growing, while the Kingdom of God is shrinking"? Have you seen that bear out in a church? What was happening?*
- *Do you truly believe that everyone has a role in building the Kingdom? Why or why not?*
- *Have you identified your unique role in Kingdom building?*
- *Why are Kingdom building and hero making inseparable from mobilization?*
- *Are you identifying and mobilizing everyday missionaries? If not, what initial steps could you lead your church to take?*
- *Are you on the path to becoming a hero maker whose fruit grows on others' trees? What actions are you taking to get there and stay there?*

HEROMAKER RESOURCES

Over the last five chapters of this book focusing on the five practices for hero making, we've offered simple and practical tools you can use to help you implement each shift in your life and ministry. We also want to give you some specific resources you and your team can use to take an even deeper dive into hero making.

Hero Maker: Five Essential Practices for Leaders to Multiply Leaders

This is the "source" book from which our other Hero Maker books are developed. This is a must-read resource on hero-making. Visit www. HeroMakerBook.org to learn more.

Free Online Hero Maker Assessment

Interested in assessing your personal multiplication leadership capacity (i.e. your "hero-making capacity")? Use this simple, FREE online tool that takes less than 30 minutes to complete. You'll get immediate results.

Visit http://church-multiplication.com/personalleadership-2/ to take the assessment.

Additional Hero Maker Resources

For additional Hero Maker Resources, including videos and podcasts on each of the hero maker practices, please go to https://exponential.org/hero-maker/.

ENDNOTES

1. *Hero Maker: Five Essential Practices for Leaders to Multiply Leaders* by Dave Ferguson and Warren Bird, 2018 (Zondervan).
2. *Halftime: Moving From Success to Significance Anniversary Edition* by Bob Buford, 2015 (Zondervan).
3. *Measure What Matters: How Google, Bono and Bill Gates Are Rocking the World With OKRs* by John Doerr and Larry Page, 2018 (Portfolio).
4. Ibid.
5. Ibid.
6. *Hero Maker.*
7. Ibid.
8. *Exponential: How You and Your Friends Can Start a Missional Church Movement* by Dave and Jon Ferguson, 2010 (Zondevan).
9. "Growing Young" study, 2016, https://churchesgrowingyoung.com/research.
10. *Halftime.*
11. *More: Find Your Personal Calling and Live Life to the Fullest Measure* by Todd Wilson, 2016 (Zondervan).
12. *Hero Maker.*
13. Ibid.
14. *More.*
15. *Hero Maker.*
16. *Hero Maker.*

ABOUT THE AUTHORS

About Dave Ferguson

Dave Ferguson is the lead pastor of Community Christian Church, an innovative multi-site missional community that is passionate about "helping people find their way back to God." Community has grown from a few college friends to thousands every weekend meeting at eleven locations in the Chicago area and has been recognized as one of America's most influential churches.

Dave provides visionary leadership for NewThing, whose mission is to be a catalyst for movements of reproducing churches. He is the president of the Exponential Conferences and the board chair for Exponential, the largest church-planting conference in the world, and is on the board of Leadership Network. He is also an adjunct professor at Wheaton Graduate School and an award-winning author of eight books, including *Hero Maker:5 Essential Practices for Leaders to Multiply Leaders*.

Dave and his wife, Sue, live in Naperville Illinois. They have three adult children, Amy, Joshua and Caleb.

About Todd Wilson

Todd Wilson is co-founder and director of Exponential (exponential.org), a community of activists devoted to church multiplication. The international organization's core focus is distributing resources for church multiplication leaders.

Todd received his B.S. in nuclear engineering from North Carolina State University and a master's degree equivalent from the Bettis Atomic Power Laboratory. For fifteen years, he served in the Division of Naval Reactors on nuclear submarine design, operation, maintenance, and overhaul.

After a two-year wrestling match with God, Todd entered full-time vocational ministry as the executive pastor at New Life Christian Church where he played a visionary and strategic role for several years as New Life grew and implemented key initiatives such as multi-site, externally focused outreach, and church planting. His passion for starting healthy new churches continues to grow. Todd now spends most of his energy engaged in a wide range of leading-edge and pioneering initiatives aimed at helping catalyze movements of healthy, multiplying churches.

Todd has written/co-written multiple books, including *Stories of Sifted* (with Eric Reiss), *Spark: Igniting a Culture of Multiplication, Becoming a Level Five Multiplying Church* (with Dave Ferguson), *Dream Big, Plan Smart* (with Will Mancini), *Multipliers: Leading Beyond Addition*, and *More: Find Your Personal Calling and Live Life to the Fullest Measure* (Zondervan Publishing).

Todd is married to Anna, and they have two adult sons who are both married — Ben to Therese; and Chris to Mariah.

ΞXPONENTIAL⌐

RESOURCING CHURCH PLANTERS

- 90+ eBooks
- Largest annual church planting conference in the world (Exponential Global Event in Orlando)
- Regional Conferences - Boise, DC, Southern CA, Bay Area CA, Chicago, Houston and New York City
- Exponential Español (spoken in Spanish)
- FREE Online Multiplication & Mobilization Assessments
- FREE Online Multiplication & Mobilization Courses
- Conference content available via Digital Access Pass (Training Videos)
- Weekly Newsletter
- 1000+ Hours of Free Audio Training
- 100s of Hours of Free Video Training
- Free Podcast Interviews

exponential.org

Twitter.com/churchplanting
Facebook.com/churchplanting
Instagram.com/church_planting

Made in the USA
Columbia, SC
01 June 2020